THE SANTA CRUZ HAGGADAH

KIDS' PASSOVER FUN BOOK

by

Karen G.R. Roekard

THE HINENI CONSCIOUSNESS PRESS
BERKELEY, CALIFORNIA

The Hineni Consciousness Press
1645 Virginia Street
Berkeley, Ca. 94703
(510) 843 - 4952

THE SANTA CRUZ HAGGADAH

Deluxe Leader's Edition:
ISBN 0-9628913-9-8

Regular Leader's Edition:
ISBN 0-9628913-4-7

Participant's Edition:
ISBN 0-9628913-8-X

KIDS' PASSOVER FUN BOOK

ISBN 0-9628913-0-4

For additional copies write or call:

The Hineni Consciousness Press
(510)843-4952

We offer significant discounts for volume purchases and welcome feedback from you.

INTRODUCTION: About this Book

This Fun Book is for people who are 'kids' or who want to honor the part of themselves that is still a kid. It has all sorts of games, puzzles, fill-ins, a maze, word games and tons of cartoons from *The Santa Cruz Haggadah* to color -- and all relate to Passover.

Because many traditional haggadot are translated directly from the Hebrew, they do not include the complete story of Passover. The story is included in this book and can be read at your Seder irrespective of the haggadah you use.

Several key details have been left out, 'voids' have been created: (1) I have found that kids whose family's tell the complete traditional Passover story, get pleasure from being able to say: "Wait a minute, where is .....?" And by doing this, what they know is then reinforced. (2) Families, and children, who don't like either the violence or, what they would term, the 'supernatural' aspects of the story, are given the space within which to create and share the key features in a manner that is congruent with their spiritual, religious and political value and belief systems. (3) Finally, I believe that the moment has been reached in Jewish history where it is critically important for us to create materials which, through their flexibility and the voids left to be filled in, are capable of being fully inclusive, of honoring everyone's versions of our story.

This would be the way of the Jewish mystical tradition, the Kabbalah, where there is a belief that the universe was formed in the void created by a contraction of the Creator's omnipresence. One of the things to learn from this is that we get creative when we have a void: the absence of that which we expect, need or hope for. My blessing for you is that you fill the spaces in your life in a joyous and creative way. Happy Passover!!

Conceived, Designed & Produced by Karen Roekard
Illustrations by Nina Paley as originally seen in The Santa Cruz Haggadah
Cover Design by Karen Roekard, Talia Cooper, Michelle Shafrir
and Sergie Loobkoff
Cover Colorizing by Sergie Loobkoff
Page Layout by Karen Roekard
Paste Up by Karen Roekard, David Cooper, Elaine Fink & Words To Go
Text, Puzzles, Games, etc. by Karen Roekard
except for the Plague Maze & Menorah Triangle Puzzle by David Jonathan
Major Kid Input from Talia Cooper & Lev Hirschhorn
Total support, encouragement & nurturing from David Cooper
including everything needed whether asked for or not

What do you call a kid who sucks up knowledge
 about Passover without even trying?
Answer: Os-Moses   David Cooper

THIS BOOK IS DEDICATED TO THREE PEOPLE WHO
SHARE WITH ME A JOY, ENERGY & LOVE THAT MUST
HAVE 'KID WISDOM' AS ITS SOURCE

DAVID COOPER, TALIA COOPER & LEV HIRSCHHORN

A long time ago when the Jewish people were called 'Hebrews,' they lived as twelve tribes of brothers and sisters.

Which line should Elijah grab to lead the parade of the Hebrew tribe's banners?

1

Finish the picture of these happy people & then color them in!

At first they were treated well and they gave thanks for their good fortune.

Many years passed. The old king of Mitzrayim, called 'Pharaoh,' died and a new Pharaoh became the ruler. He didn't like the Hebrew tribes.

First he put their leaders into jail

4

They worked for Pharaoh very very hard until finally a man named Moses became the leader of the Hebrews. He wanted Pharaoh to let the people go free.

Can you figure out which two of these slaves are the same?

6

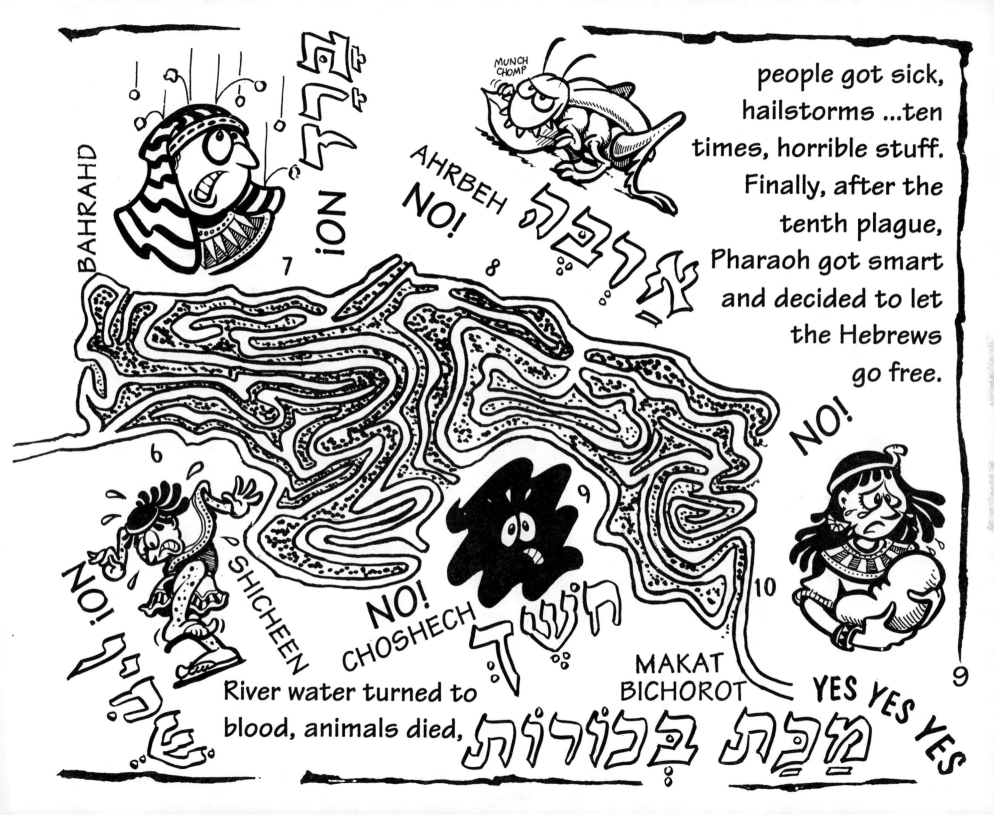

They raced out of Mitzrayim through the Red Sea

Race to Freedom! Make a path through the house and time each person as they run the course. Then do it on one foot, holding hands, etc.

to freedom.

Most of the people danced and were happy

because they no longer had to be slaves!

SKIP SKIP SKIP

Finish this picture to find the animal who jumped for joy.

11

On a more personal note, others had a different response:

Case #1: Hymie,
the taskmaster -

Case #2: Schlemeel,
the unprepared -

Schlemeel is so unprepared, he can't figure out which is his shadow. Can you?

He was very unhappy
because now he was out of a job.

He was embarassed
because when the call came
to leave he wasn't ready.

So that is the story of how the Hebrew Tribes were freed from slavery. We remember the day of their freedom by celebrating a holiday called **Passover.**

Draw a picture of what freedom looks like to you!

14

ULC
ACH
ZEE
ADE
IRT
AGG
LEL
KOR
RPA
RAC
TZA
ARO
ARE
ZAH
HAT

Help the people make a seder by filling in the correct 3 letters into each word on the left. Then say each one out loud.

K _ _ SH _ _ Z
U'REC _ _ _
KA _ _ _ S _
Y _ _ _ ATZ
M _ _ _ ID
_ _ _ HTZAH
MŌET
MAT _ _ R
M _ _ ECH
SH _ _ HAN ORECH
_ _ _ FFUN
B _ _ CH
HAL _ _ _
N _ _ ZAH

Each year at Passover time
we make a special get-together
called a 'seder' where we tell
the story of Pharaoh and Moses
and being slaves and being freed.
We eat different foods and do
all kinds of interesting things.
And we do it today just like the
people who came before us did
it for thousands of years.

15

In the middle of the table there is a special plate called 'the seder plate' on which there are all kinds of unusual things to look at and to eat.

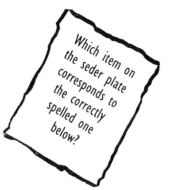

Which item on the seder plate corresponds to the correctly spelled one below?

GG E

HANKS BONE

PAS ARK

R MARO

ROSES CHA

RESZE CHA

EGG
CHAZERES
KARPAS
SHANKBONE
CHAROSES
MAROR

Fill in only the triangles to see what they are lighting. What's it called?

Just like on Sabbath and other Jewish holidays, the first thing to do is to light candles.

Study the seder plate on page 16. How many of the things on the plate can you remember!

...FOR THOSE WHO CAN LOVE...FOR THOSE WHO FEEL EMPTY...FOR THOSE NOT YET BORN...FOR THOSE WHO ARE IN TOUCH WITH THEIR MINDS......WHO ARE GETTING IN TOUCH WITH THEIR BODIES...

Then there are a whole bunch of things we do to remind us of the Hebrew slaves who became free.

u'rechatz
wash hands

וּרְחַץ

kadesh
drink wine

קַדֵּשׁ

Color in the stained glass as follows:
1=dark blue 2=tan
3=light blue
4=yellow 5=orange
6= purple

18

karpas

יַחַץ

More people at the seder than expected. Need another piece of Karpas. Copy the picture into the adjacent grid.

yachatz

There are five afikomans hidden in this book. They look like this half of the matzah. Can you find them?

כַּרְפַּס

eat fruit of the earth

break middle matzah

ACROSS

1 What the salt water reminds us of
4 Hebrew midwife who saved the babies
5 Passover bread
7 You get a present if you find it
10 Mitzrim suffered through 10 of these
11 The number of cups of wine we drink at a seder
12 Bitter herb
13 Holiday name

DOWN

2 Open the door for this prophet.
3 A _ _ _ _ _ must do what the master says.
4 King of the Mitzrim.
6 She led the women in dance at the sea.
8 Greens on the Seder plate.
9 He was one of the Hebrews' leaders.
11 When they left Mitzrayim the Hebrews were _ _ _ _ _ .

Can you complete this Passover crossword puzzle?

maggid

מַגִּיד

tell story

Can you figure out which adult each of these kids grew up to be?

rachtzah

רָחְצָה

wash hands

What's wrong with this picture?

SLURRRP!

moetzee matzah

מוֹצִיא מַצָּה

honor matzah

maror

מָרוֹר

eat bitter herbs

korech כורך
eat a combination of
matzah, maror & charoset

shulchan orech שׁלחן עורך
CHOMP!

Finish the pictures;
all lines should be
solid. Then draw in
a picture of the
'right' food they
should be eating.

tzaffun צפון
find & eat the afikoman

barech ברך
say 'thank you' for food

22

hallel

הַלֵּל

give praise

Fill this page with foot-prints. Make up stories about why there are 2 sets of footprints and only one person?

nirtzah

נִרְצָה

ask for acceptance

23

Every now and then a new 'Pharaoh' in a different country comes into power who wants to do something bad to the people of that country.

Find the **10** shankbones. Some are obvious and some are not!

It is our job to remember the story of Pharaoh and Moses and the plagues and being freed from being slaves. Then we will always

remember

to fight for our rights and our freedom from whoever is being mean to us or to anybody else.

```
L T H A Z T H C A R H M Y N
K E A N N Z K H M A G G I D
A O L H O I A L O S B M T I
D E R L L Y R O E S A H Z G
E N O E A T P T T T R T A C
S U R E C H A T Z Z E M F H
H R A V A H S A E A C M F S
K S M K O R H C E H H K U A
H Z Z H A S H U L C H A N H
T Z T A H C A Y O R E C H T
```

KADESH
U'RECHATZ
KARPAS
YACHATZ
MAGGID
RACHTZAH
MOETZEE
MATZAH
MAROR
KORECH
SHULCHAN ORECH
TZAFFUN
BARECH
HALLEL
NIRTZAH

Can you find the names of the rituals. Try horizontal, vertical, backwards, forwards, and diagonal.

BIFF!

Make your own haggadah. Put the pieces on page 27 into their corresponding box on this page.

And everything we need to remember is written down in a very special book called a 'haggadah.' It comes in many versions so find one that you like or WRITE YOUR OWN.

HAPPY PASSOVER!!!!!

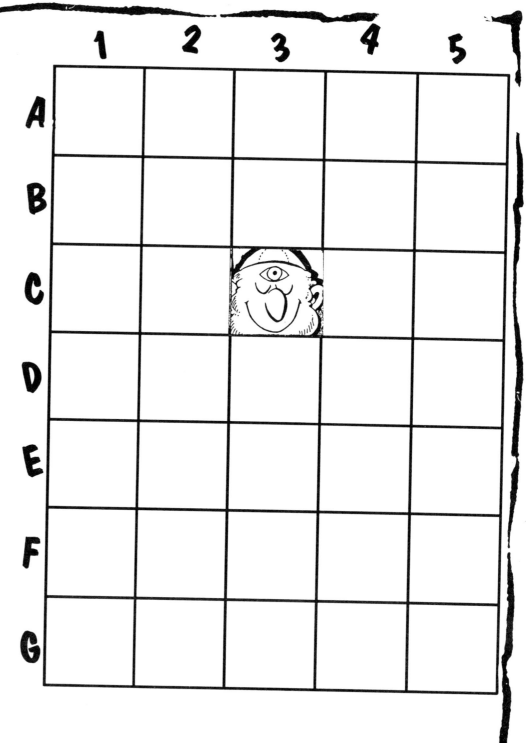

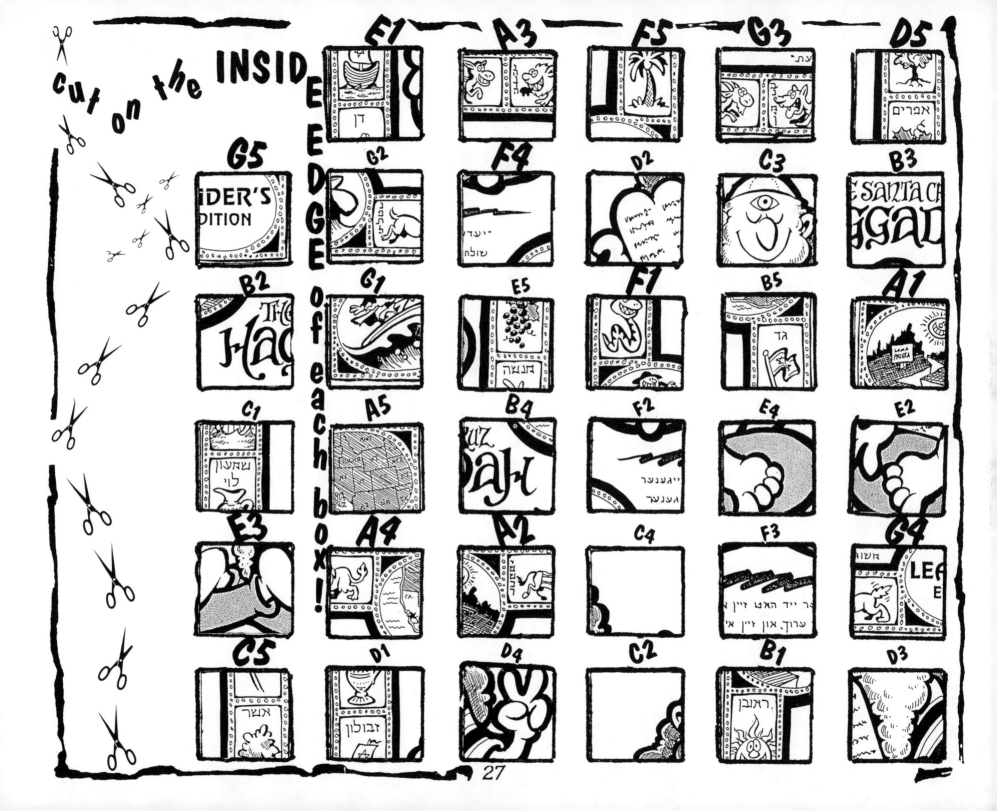

These pages are for making a drawing and coloring record of everything that is happening around your house and your school for Passover. You can also use them for making decorations and invitations.

ANSWERS:

Page 1: D

Page 2: A = regular hello B = peace symbol greeting C = Jewish priestly blessing & Star Trek greeting

Page 6: B & D

Page 7: "If you don't let my people go, you'll be sorry!!

Page 11: Ram

Page 12: 3

Page 18: A picture of a pitcher pouring water over hands

Page 20: I don't know; your guess is as good as mine

Hidden Afikomans: P2: in dog; p4: in hat on left; p8: to the right of 'Dom'; p.15: under word 'Passover'; p.26: above word 'Passover.'

Page 15:

K_ADE_SH
U'REC_HAT_Z
KA_RPA_S
Y_ACH_ATZ
M_AGG_ID
_RAC_HTZAH
MOET_ZEE
MAT_ZAH
M_ARO_R
KOR_ECH
SH_ULC_HAN ORECH
TZA_FFUN
B_ARE_CH
HAL_LEL_
N_IRT_ZAH

Page 17:

Page 19:

crossword:

T	E	A	R	S													
E				L				P	U	A	H						
L				A		M	A	T	Z	A	H					M	
I				V				A	F	I	K	O	M	A	N	I	
J								R		A	O			F	O	U	R
P	L	A	G	U	E	S		A		R	S	E		R		I	
H								M	A	R	O	R		E		A	
								O		P	S					M	
								H		P	A	S	S	O	V	E	R

Page 8/9:

AHROVE

DEHVER

KEENIM
NO!

NO!

NO!

NO!

ION

ION

AHRBEH
NO!

SHICHEEN

NO!
CHOSHECH

NO!

MAKAT BICHOROT

YES YES YES

NO!

Page 26/27:

Page 25:

Additional STUFF TO DO:
some of it may require help from your teachers or parents!

ACTIVITIES: **Before Seder** (and many that continue into the seder):

* TAPE OF FAMILY:

* Make a tape, audio or video, for family members who will not be at your seder - sing songs, tell stories, show them that you care and will miss their presence.

* DECORATIONS FOR THE SEDER:

GENERAL DECORATIONS:

* Mobiles - (1) take the cartoons of the plagues, color them and paste them onto cardboard. Get a wooden embroidery ring and string the cardboard pieces to it. Hang it over the table. Have the younger kids point to the correct plague as they are called out; ask the older kids what they consider to be modern day plagues, e.g. pollution. (2) Xerox two copies of each of the cartoon banners of the Hebrew tribes who left Mitzrayim. Paste them onto paper cups, closest to the edge where your mouth goes. String the cups together by making a hole through their center. These can either be hung above the table or laid on the table.

* Felt pictures - trace a cartoon from this book onto a large piece of felt. Now cut out other pieces of colored felt to create a picture to suit your taste. Hang it up.

TABLE DECORATIONS:

* 'The Animals Who Left Mitzrayim' -(1) Use potatoes or some other sturdy fruit or vegetable for the body and small pieces for the head, legs and tails and make animals out of vegetables. Make up a story to go with each animal. Decorate the seder with the animals. Have the kids make up a story about each animal. (2) Carve a bar of soap into the 'animals' you think left Mitzrayim. Use the soap to wash hands before eating.

* Painted Rocks - Choose flat rocks and paint the entire rock the color you want. Let it dry and then paint the words: "I AM A SLAVE!" on one side and "I AM FREE" on the other. Start the Seder with the side that says 'Slave' facing up. Turn it over when the story talks about the Hebrews becoming free.

* Placemats - Trace cartoons from this book onto xerox paper. Color the cartoons and give each person their own unique placemat.

* Bookmarks - Shrink your favorite cartoons or other picture onto xerox paper. Then cut them out or trace them onto pieces of cardboard or felt. Color them in. Make one for each person attending your seder to use to mark their place in their haggadah when the meal break comes.

DECORATED SEDER PLATES:

* Paper mache Seder plate - take a large flat plate, protect it with plastic wrap and/or petroleum jelly and cover it with six or seven layers of wet newspaper strips dipped in wallpaper paste. Let dry and separate new plate from original one. Use the cartoon of the seder plate as a model and paint the new plate with tempura or poster paints. Varnish. (Can also make a matzah plate this way!)

* Painted Seder plate - Using a white glazed china plate, trace the cartoon seder plate onto it. Paint the outline first; let dry. Then do the background color; let dry. Finish painting the plate. (Can also make a matzah plate or a set of Passover dishes).

Put the kids seder plates in a special place on the table!

* Shankbone substitute - for anyone who cannot get, or does not want to use, a real shankbone, make one out of baked and painted clay or paper mache. Some people are now using a yam as a representative of the Passover 'yam' as opposed to 'lamb.' Another advantage of using a yam is that you can then play 'hot yam' instead of 'hot potato.'

WINDOW DECORATIONS:

* Have kids color in pictures from the haggadah. Paste them, facing out, in your windows.

HANGING DECORATIONS:

* Passover paper chain - Divide a piece of xerox paper into four or five columns. Draw pictures of the people and animals leaving Mitzrayim. Xerox several times. Cut strips. Loop and tape the strips together. Hang them in the room where the seder will be.

PILLOW COVER DECORATIONS:

* Trace cartoons from this book onto pillow covers. Paint in the pictures using either magic marker or paints. Put a covered pillow at each attendees place so that they remember that now they are to be free.

INVITATIONS:

Xerox your favorite cartoons and make them into seder invitations, Passover cards, placecards or thank you cards. Color them in before you send them.

INSTRUMENTS:

Make instruments to be used along with the songs - make enough for everyone attending - tambourines, out of aluminum pie plates stapled together; rattles, out of plastic bottles filled with pebbles; drums out of small boxes. Make sure to color or paint these to make them look pretty.

ACCESSORIES:

* Scarves for scarf dancing - Paint or batik a long piece of fabric with beautiful colors and designs. At the seder, when the part comes that the Hebrews are freed, you can use the scarves to create a family dance like Miriam and the women did at the Red Sea.

WORD GAMES:

* True/false - Take the Passover story and make up a version that has ridiculous possibilities for true/false responses throughout. For example: "12 yellow submarines went down to Nigeria because the sea caved in: True/False. With little kids, you the

storyteller keeps reading and asking "True/False." With older kids, if they answer 'false', ask them to give you the right answer. You can set up a scoring system if you want.

* Mad-Libs - prepare a version of the Passover story where you have deleted names, geographic locations, parts of speech, food, thing, etc. At the seder everyone can play and then you can read aloud the story you all created.

STORY MAKING:

*Prepare a script to put on a Passover play of the story of Passover - (1) make costumes so you can dress up as the characters (2) instead of dressing up, make a special hat for each character (3) or prepare puppets made out of something like painted boxes, socks, bags, toilet paper rolls or anything else you can think of. Put on a performance at the seder of the script you have prepared.

* Draw and paint Pharaoh on one paper plate and Moses on another.

* Write a story about any of the ritual objects we use on Passover, e.g. The Matzah Who Wouldn't Break, The Angry Maror and How He Got Sweet, etc. Tell the story at the seder when that ritual is done.

PUZZLES:

* Xerox cartoons from this book, attach them to cardboard and then cut them up into a puzzle. You can use either of the covers of this book to do that as well!.

CREATING MEMORIES:

* Creating yearly 'life portraits' - buy a roll of paper that is at least three feet wide. Have kids lie down on it and make an outline of their body. During the seder have them fill in the parts of their face and then put arrows to indicate the parts of their body that they are focusing on this year, e.g. arms for playing baseball - they can then draw in the baseball. They (or you if they don't yet write) can list their favorite activities, friends, etc. ...the aspects of their life that are important to them at that Passover. If you do this every year or even some of years, then at the time of their Bar or Bat Mitzvah you will be able to hang these life portraits up and see a progression.

COOKING:
* Boil & Peel the eggs - great for any age kid.
* Cut up and boil potatoes to use as Karpas.
* Grate horseradish - for older kids only as this stings eyes.
* Make Charoset - usually a combination of apples, nuts, wine & spices. Best to consult a Jewish cookbook so that you can give an explicit recipe of your favorite version to your kids to make.
 GIVE THEM RESPONSIBILITY; they'll feel more a part of things!!!!

CREATE A HAGGADAH OR SOME PART OF ONE:
* Many families are dissatisfied with the versions of the haggadah that they have available to them from their local booksellers. Also, as kids grow up, the needs of families at seders change. It is a wonderful practice to create your own haggadah yearly as your needs change. And it is a great assignment to give 'middle aged' kids a section to make the decision on, like which version of the story to tell and several haggadot to choose from. You can assign every attendee a section to choose and then make your own haggadah from out of their choices.

You should try to have a representative from each of the three traditions of haggadah so that your haggadah writers will have what to choose from. They are:(1) the traditional ones - they focus on looking backward to 'Egypt' and the exodus to get the Passover sense of slavery and liberation. Most haggadot are in this category. (2) the political haggadot - these focus on looking outward to some form of 'tikun olam,' the healing of the planet: via civil rights, feminism, gay rights, vegetarianism, etc. There is a political haggadah available for virtually every interest group. (3) the psycho-spiritual - these focus on having the major focus be to look inward, to ask the question: "How do I enslave myself? How do I hold myself back? How can I free myself from my self-generated enslavement? If there is no bookstore in your area that carries a full range of haggadot, then you can always call one of the major bookstores in a given region. For example, here in Berkeley, Afikomen (our Judaica store) and Cody's (a large secular store) each carry over 100 haggadot before Passover. I am sure there are equivalent stores all over the country and if not, both Afikomen & Cody's ship.

Activities: **DURING THE SEDER**

CREATING THE MAGIC OF PASSOVER:
* What our ancestors did in creating the seder was attempt to set up a special situation of an almost magical quality -- foods suddenly stood for things other than themselves, they would be eaten out of the normal order, there would be set talking before eating, reclining instead of sitting, etc. They were brilliant at creating a situation that for the year 300 or 800 or 1300 or even 1800AD was probably mesmorizing. We of the technological age need to work harder to create the magic that will get and retain kids attention. You know your kids, (hopefully), and what gets their attention. You know yourself, (hopefully), so you know what you can do that would be different from what you normally do and thus, get their attention. If you never eat by candle-light, do that. If you are the one who usually directs the meals, assign someone else at least a section of it. Start talking aboutthe holiday well in advance of it so that there is a build up. Do a massive 'spring/Passover' house cleaning and save crumbs of bread. Have everyone gather early in the morning of the first seder and do the ritual of the burning of the leaven - 'bidikot chometz' - so that the specialness of the holiday and the upcoming seder is imprinted in them. GIVE THEM A SIGNIFICANT PART IN THE SEDER!!! Publicly acknowledge them and anything they have done for the seder - our ancestors knew the importance of focussing on the children to connect them to what was important to them. Kids love 'secret ceremonies.' Use them as a model.

* Embodying the seder - kids often connect through their senses (so do we but they are less distracted by intellect and super-ego!). Take the concepts of the seder and find ways to connect them to the senses more. For example: When talking about slavery and freedom, have a big person hold a little person real tight so that they cannot move. Ask them what it feels like. Have them say: "Let me GO!!!" Ask them what that feels like. Then free them; how does that feel.

* Politicize the Seder - If you use a traditional haggadah, at various points ask what the concepts mean today from the political perspective, for example: "What are the plagues we live with today? What groups are still needing to get free? Are the people in some other country in the world who live within a dictatorship, are they some form of slaves? What are the rights of animals? etc."

* Psycho-spiritualize the Seder - I won't get into this heavily here because my haggadah, The Santa Cruz Haggadah - Leader's Version, has 36 questions that look to the seder from the perspective of 'How do I enslave myself? How do I hold myself back with the words I don't say, the repetitive actions I take, the belief systems I hold ("Oh, I couldn't do that!"), etc.

KIDS FUN BOOK:

* If your kids are not kids who enjoy sitting at a seder, and if they will be disruptive to everyone's else's enjoyment, then LET THEM USE THIS BOOK TO ENTERTAIN THEMSELVES WHILE CONNECTING WITH PASSOVER AND WHAT IS HAPPENNING AT 'SEDER CENTER.'

REVERSE RITUAL:

* If possible, maybe for the second seder, turn things completely around and have the kids run the show, choose how much is read, who reads, etc.

ACTIVITIES:

* Reporters - Have each of the kids at the first seder be a 'newspaper reporter,' e.g. Clark Kent & Lois Lane. Give them pads to write in and have them take notes on

everything they see, hear, smell, jokes told, who'se there, what they wore, etc. Give them the reporting assignment and have them share their notes at the second night seder.

* Make an 'Attendee Tree' - Trace the hands of each attendee at the seder, using green paper for relatives and yellow or red paper for friends. Write their names on their hand tracings. Take a piece of construction paper and draw the trunk of a tree and branches. Paste the green hands on to the tree in the right place - the oldest generation at the top and working downward. Add the yellow or red hands around the tree. Put up on the wall next year and see what has changed.

TALKING GAMES:

* "I Spy With My Little Eye" - can play this with all the items on the table.

* "When the Hebrews left Mitzrayim" - you finish the sentence with something they did. . e.g. danced, laughed. Go around the table and each person has to remember what the people before them suggested and then has to do all the things that came before and add one.

* "Pass the _____" - start a fantasy story about one of the ritual objects on the table and stop at a critical moment and tap the person next to you.

* Silly Seder - Cut out the Hebrew names of the rituals and put them in a hat. Pick one out at a time and tell what it is. You can also laythem out on the table and try to get them in the right order.

* Discussions of G-d & where the plagues came from - I have deliberately chosen to make this book 'G-d neutral' & 'explanation of the plagues neutral.' Everyone has their own sense of 'breath of holy' and of where the plagues came from and what they are. I leave the privilege of these explanations to each kid's parents or significant person.

* Concepts games - Take the concepts of Passover and ask kids what they might mean to us today - see above.

ACTING GAMES:
   Take the song 'Chad Gadya' or Echad Me Yoda'ah' and act out what is happenning.

PLEASE WRITE AND LET ME KNOW   Karen Roekard
ABOUT ANY GAMES, PUZZLES, ETC.   1645 Virginia Street
YOU DO FOR PASSOVER !!!   Berkeley, Ca. 94703 USA